Razzle-Dazzle Riddles

by Giulio Maestro

CLARION BOOKS

TICKNOR & FIELDS: A HOUGHTON MIFFLIN COMPANY

NEW YORK

Clarion Books
Ticknor & Fields, a Houghton Mifflin Company

Library of Congress Cataloging in Publication Data
Maestro, Giulio.
Razzle-dazzle riddles.
Summary: Sixty-one original riddles created and
illustrated by the author.
1. Riddles, Juvenile. [1. Riddles] I. Title.
PN6371.5.M285   1985   818'.5402   85-3785
ISBN 0-89919-382-X   PA ISBN 0-89919-405-2

BD 10 9 8 7 6 5 4 3 2 1

★Razzle-Dazzle★
★Riddles★

Where do pearls sleep?

In an oyster bed.

What is a stonecutter's favorite dessert?

Marble cake.

What do you call a hot pepper in winter?

A chilly chili.

Why did the ghost look so thin?

He was just a shadow of his former self.

What's a bear's hat at the North Pole?

A polar ice cap.

When does a hawk pick new team players?

When she's a talon scout.

What did one bush say to the other one?

"I know yew!"

What is a chubby Christmas dessert?

Plump pudding.

Why does a skeleton have a bad memory?

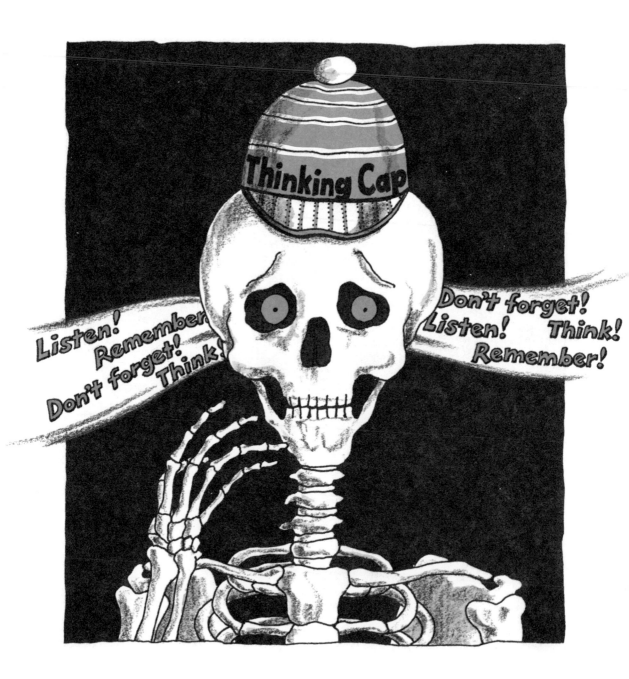

Words go in one ear and out the other.

Why did the giant get lost?

His head was always in the clouds.

Why did the tree get so many phone calls?

He was poplar.

What is a baby apple seed?

A pip-squeak.

What is a solar hat?

A sunbonnet.

What gives a ghost the right to scare you?

A haunting license.

Why did the cook hurry to the herb garden?

He hadn't much thyme.

Why did the tailor seem so nervous?

He was always on pins and needles.

What's a weekend dessert?

A Sunday sundae.

Why was the car dressed up in a
ghost costume?

It wanted to get into the Halloween spirit.

When is a tree like a king's hand?

When it's a royal palm.

Why were the eggs so excited?

They couldn't wait to get cracking!

Why were the bones chasing the skull?

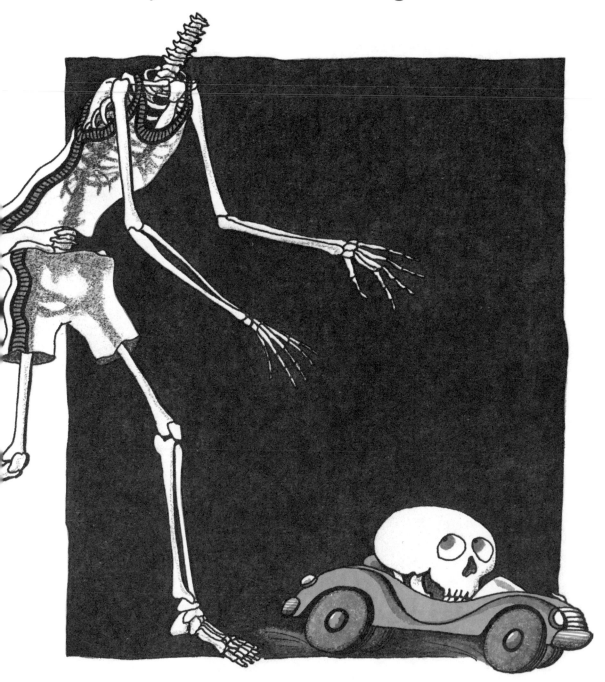

They wanted to get ahead.

Why is it depressing to step into quicksand?

You get a sinking feeling.

Why was the sponge so tired?

It was wiped out.

What is a feathered prisoner?

A jailbird.

How does a ghost open a heavy door?

With deadly force.

What's a big wheel for a big wheel?

A unicycle that's fit for a king.

Who does a goblin take out on a date?

His ghoulfriend.

Why are horses good dancers?

They're natural hoofers.

When do slices of bread ride in a
patrol boat?

When they're in the toast guard.

Why didn't the bird eat the farmhouse?

She was a barn swallow.

When is a tree not very tasty?

When it's yucca.

How does a witch keep her door locked?

With a deadbolt.

Why was the guitar so irritable?

It was fretful.

What is a shellfish disaster?

A clamity.

When is a balloon depressed?

When it's deflated.

How does a witch keep her ears warm?

She wears eerie muffs.

What's a strong sled dog?

A husky husky.

Why did the engineer dream about
her train?

She had a one-track mind.

What do you call a very small queen?

Your Royal Lowness.

Why was the herb so wise?

It was sage.

What do you call a ghost's middle?

Dead center.

How does a cat keep his breath fresh?

With mousewash.

How are sausages like a chain?

They're linked.

What is a ghostly police officer?

A Detective Inspecter.

What does a noisy plane do when it takes off?

It raises a racket.

When does a baseball belong at a
masquerade party?

When it's a masked ball.

How does an evergreen tree keep its
hair neat?

It uses a pinecomb.

Why did the grizzly buy a pair of shoes?

He had bear feet.

Why did the skeleton need a good night's sleep?

She was bone-weary.

What is a puppy on a mountain peak?

Top dog.

Why did Triceratops go to the doctor?

He had a dino sore.

How can you get a tan in a tree?

Sun yourself on a beech.

Why shouldn't you add too many numbers on a hot day?

You might get sumstroke.

What is the opposite of an uneducated
pearl?

A cultured one.

Why did the birds shine a flashlight
on their nest?

To have beacon and eggs.

What is a cracked rock with no money?

Stone-broke.

Why did the thread tell jokes to the needle?

To keep it in stitches.

Why does a ghost write in code?

To be cryptic.

What did the young sapling grow to be?

Alder and wiser.

When is a snug muffler like a snake?

When it's a boa.

What kind of jokes does a wolf like?

Howlers!